Richard Scarry's
MR. FRUMBLE'S COFFEE SHOP DISASTER

A GOLDEN BOOK • NEW YORK

Western Publishing Company, Inc., Racine, Wisconsin 53404

 Library of Congress Catalog Card Number: 93-78416 ISBN: 0-307-30141-9 MCMXCV

Mr. Frumble takes a walk through Busytown.
He buys himself a newspaper.

He reads it while he walks.
Please watch where you
are going, Mr. Frumble!

SPLISH!

SPLOTCH!

Mr. Frumble falls into wet cement.
Now he needs a new suit.

Mr. Frumble goes to the tailor.

He tries on a new suit.
RIPPP! go the stitches.
Please be careful, Mr. Frumble.

Wearing his new suit,
Mr. Frumble leaves the tailor.
The wind blows off his hat.

It lands in sticky street tar.
Watch your step, Mr. Frumble!

ZLIP! ZWATCH!
Poor Mr. Frumble!
Poor new suit!

Mr. Frumble needs a rest. He
goes to Mr. Raccoon's Coffee Shop.

He sits down on a stool and asks
Mr. Raccoon for a glass of milk.

"Mr. Frumble, could you please look after the shop for five minutes?" says Mr. Raccoon. "I have to go to the bank for a roll of coins."

Uh-oh. Mr. Raccoon, I don't think that is a very good idea!

As soon as Mr. Raccoon goes out, Hilda Hippo comes in. Mr. Frumble politely gets up from his stool. RIPPP! go his pants.

Mr. Frumble runs quickly behind the counter.

"I'm so thirsty from shopping, I need something to drink," says Hilda.

Mr. Frumble offers her a glass of water. He tries to turn on the tap, but it comes off in his hand. SWUSH!

Hilda runs away screaming.

Across the street at the bank, Mr. Raccoon waits his turn in line.

At the Coffee Shop, Mr. Frumble plugs the water spout with a rag. Then he goes to look for a mop.

There are many customers ahead of him.

He opens a door.
It is the refrigerator door. Inside he finds some ice cream.

"Mmmm!" he says, placing the box on the stove.

Just as Mr. Frumble finds the mop,
he knocks over a stack of plates.
CRASH!
Oh, dear! The ice cream is
melting. It's running down
the front of the stove.

At the bank, it is Mr. Raccoon's turn at the window
at last. But just as he gets there, the window closes.

He goes to
another line.

Then Bananas Gorilla
enters the Coffee Shop.

Bananas wades through
the water, ice cream, and
broken plates. "I just have
to have a banana milk shake!"
he says.

Mr. Frumble peels some bananas and puts them in the mixer.

But he can't find the cover for the machine.
He switches on the mixer anyway.

WWRRR! FLITCH! FLATCH!
Bits of banana fly everywhere.
They stick to everything, even the ceiling!
Bananas Gorilla is terrified! He runs away.

"Dear me! I'd better clean this up before
Mr. Raccoon comes back!" Mr. Frumble says.
He climbs up a ladder with the mop to
wipe the pieces of banana from the ceiling.

Be careful, Mr. Frumble!
WHOOPS!
Mr. Frumble grabs the
window curtains.
RIP!
Down come the curtains.
CRASH!
Down comes Mr. Frumble.

At long last Mr. Raccoon gets his roll of coins from the bank.

"I certainly wasn't very lucky at the bank today!" he says to himself.

"Poor Mr. Frumble. I hope he didn't mind waiting so long for me in the Coffee Shop."

I don't think Mr. Raccoon knows just
how unlucky he has been today, do you?